NUMBER ONE NORTHERN. Variety: Marquis or any variety equal to Marquis. Well matured, practically free from damaged kernels. Maximum limits of foreign material other than wheat: practically free from matter other than cereal grains. Maximum limits of wheats of other classes or varieties: practically free from Durham; total including Durham: about 1%. Minimum weight per measured bushel, 60 lbs.

NUMBER ONE NORTHERN

EDITED BY
ROBERT CURRIE GARY HYLAND
BARBARA SAPERGIA GEOFFREY URSELL

POETRY FROM SASKATCHEWAN

Cover and title page design by Bill Johnson.

Photographs of Saskatchewan places and people by Richard Gustin.

Excerpts from a letter to the Saskatchewan Wheat Pool courtesy of the Saskatchewan Wheat Pool. Thanks to Liz Hilts for her assistance.

ISBN 0-919926-04-5

Published with the assistance of the Canada Council and the Saskatchewan Arts Board.

Thunder Creek Publishing Co-operative Limited
1188 Duffield Crescent
Moose Jaw, Saskatchewan

Commercial Printers Limited

TO SASKATCHEWAN POOL ELEVATORS LIMITED,
REGINA, SASK.

March
5th
1928

In the first place I learned to grade grain in my hand and I never attempt to grade any other way. I take a sample from a load by plunging my hand right into it about up to the elbow. This sample I take to the door leading to my Office, which faces West; in the summer if the sun happens to be in the West, then to my out-drive doors which face North. I then run the grain slowly from my right hand to my left, then back again. If I am still doubtful of the grade I repeat the process.

When dumping the load I always take out the end-gate myself, and as the load runs out run my hand to and fro, throwing the different samples on the lid of the pit. I can then tell if the load is uniform. I always try to make sure to elevate the load to the right bin. The value of doing this cannot be over-estimated.

Whether my methods will meet with your approval I do not know, but I lost my first actual grade on a car this year, and have only gained four in three years. I do not think that this is bad in three years' buying with very little special-binning.

In closing I would like to add that I keep in touch with the Inspection Department by sending samples.

Yours very truly,
SASKATCHEWAN POOL ELEVATOR AGENT
FORWARD, SASK.

CONTENTS

Andrew Suknaski

INDIAN RINGS ON THE EDGE OF TONITA PASTURE

the meadow lark's song proclaiming spring
waters lazily flowing from wood mountain peat moss springs
becoming five mile creek running north
through this coulee
where i caught fish and swam in boyhood unaware
of three indian rings that nearly vanished
beneath dust from a field
lee soparlo's father worked
trying to feed his family in the thirties – this
and standing here now in this great centre ring
where something holds
me around the heart the way
the wired stone anchors a cornerpost of the nearby fence
stretching north
and west to the village where i grew up – i claim these things
my ancestral space to move through and beyond
chronicling the meaning of these vast plains
in a geography of blood
and failure
making them live

DUNC AND BABE MCPHERSON

we notice so little in our lives
i think
looking again at their photograph taken
that sunday afternoon last fall
they standing arm in arm before the flower box
nailed beneath the window
and they cast a single shadow across the wall where
the washtub hangs next to the hammer on a nail –
i now notice in the foreground
the large flat stones half the length of a man
and try to imagine the energy it took to place them there
(something in the picture turns the mind to the visit
and how we entered their house – dunc saying:
the smell of your pipe makes me lonely for the old days
when i smoked my pipes

sitting down in his easy chair
dunc gazed a moment at the floating particles moving
through a light shaft angling down to the floor –
then he recalled their first experiences
when he and philip well were blacksmiths east of the old post:
i was shaping shoes when i heard horses whinnying
i looked up and there was babe
holding the reins of her father's team
that moment i said to myself "this lil lady's my wife"
and i tell you the honest God's truth andy
i've never looked at another woman since – yes
it was pure and simple as that
babe chuckled while she poured coffee: *yes and*
i was so afraid of him then
all i could say was "my daddy wants you to shoe these horses
please."

dunc talked about tire crimping the old forgotten craft
and the way he heated iron tires red hot
to crimp them with the two huge vices
how in busy times babe often helped him
throw the hot metal rings back
on wooden wheels
suddenly immersed in a water trough to keep the wood from
  burning
dunc remembered how once a year
news arrived about a certain horserancher coming to have
his team shod:
they would jump half their height straight in the air –
the night before he arrived
i smoked myself hoarse andy and i even loaded a pipe
to calm myself in the middle of the night
when i woke up shaking from nightmares about them
dunc compares shoeing horses to tuning a banjo
and says one can tell by the sound of the nail
if one is doing it wrong and hurting the horse)

returning to their photograph
i notice how the garden has been extended
beyond the old fashioned well
note how they extended their boundaries
to include the abandoned house turned into a guest house
and i praise their full happy life here
where they found everything they ever needed
here in wood mountain where the stars are still distinct

JIMMY HOY'S PLACE

gee clyz
all time slem ting hoy would say
when he got mad at some obnoxious drunk
stirring hell in the cafe

all time takkie too much
makkie trouble sunna bitch
wadda hell madder wid you?

gee clyz hoy would mutter and scold the man
would shake his small grey head and disappear into
the smoky kitchen to scramble some eggs for the drunk

gee clyz
all time slem ting something would whisper
in the back of hoy's mind
as he sat and smoked his pipe through the long afternoons
in the empty cafe
maybe immersed in a dream where the years became centuries till
a child's coin rapped on the scratched counter
drew hoy from his dream

hoy's early history is uncertain
though some speak of a time when he first arrived at
the old post and built a small cafe and livery stable
and how drunk halfbreeds often rode into the hamlet
to lift hoy onto a table and make him dance
as they shot up the floor

when the railroad came through
and the hamlet was moved five miles north
hoy built a big new cafe complete with false front
the text reading:
HOTEL
wood mountain cafe & confectionery

back in the thirties
hoy threw hank snow out for creating a disturbance
snow had hopped off a freight
thinking a song might rustle up some food in hoy's place –
seems hoy was a bit thin himself and the song nothing new
so he escorted snow to the door
saying: *gee clyz*
all time slem ting

hoy's place was where men drank coffee and told stories
like the one about the time charlie bloiun handled
the village's only holdup
how a killdeer cowboy saw one western too many
and thought he might rob bloiun's store –
following an afternoon of beer in the west central
the man got his shotgun and tied a hanky around his face
and entered the store
while old bloiun counted his money
and whispered: *stickum up*
bloiun briefly pausing to look over his glasses
long enough to say: *pete – you better put that gun down*
before you hurt yourself
and then continued his counting while pete crept out
somewhat embarrassed

hoy's place was where in boyhood one came to know death
when men ceased joking
as someone arrived with first news of men like the jealous agent
from another town –
how he imagined a lover for his beautiful faithful wife
until one day he left a note on the grain scales
saying: *i think it'll be better this way for all of us*
and then walked his .22 behind the elevator
to perform what some believe is the most creative act

hoy's icecream and chinese calendar girls were something to dream
about
on hot july days of summerfallowing
were something to remember as one woke falling
against the twisted wheel of lovenzanna's tractor

FATHER

arrives in moose jaw fall of 1914
to find the landtitles office
is given the co-ordinates for the homestead east
of wood mountain village –
and he buys packsack and provisions for the long walk south
sleeps in haystacks for the first few nights
(finally arriving in limerick
buys homesteader's essentials: axe saw hammer
lumber nails shovel gun bullets food
and other miscellaneous items)
he hires someone with a wagon and horses
to drive him to the homestead
builds a floor and raises one wall that day
and feeling the late autumn cold
nails together a narrow box in which to sleep
the first night

the following morning
he rises through two feet of snow to find
all his tools stolen (except for the gun bullets
and knife he slept with)
he searches for a spot on the hillside
to carve out with a blunted knife
a cellar
in which to endure the first few years –
he nails together a roof with a stone

philip well is his closest neighbour
and they hunt together
and through long evenings
play cards by light of the coaloil lamp
spin tales of old country wanderings
to survive 40 below winters till pre-emption time
is up

when the landtitle is secured
and a more suitable shack is built –
father walks six times between moose jaw and
the homestead
till haggling civil bastards give him the title
each time
he carries a $10. bill sewn inside his pocket across
the heart

DIRTY THIRTIES, BURN LIGNITE COAL LIKE HELL

"morton . . .
don't you bring home anymore'ah that
cheap litnite . . . allah keep doin
is carryin out th ieshes"
– morton tucker's mother

1

one cole winner night
gunner folgerburg
never did get tah bed
jus kept shovelin that litnite
inna stove

cum mornin . . . thought'ed warm up his feet
opened up thee oven ta puddem in
n there was thee ole tomcat justta shiverin
even'iz whiskers was all froze up

2

ole gunner ustta say
"threw a sackka litnite on ma back
n ran roun th house all night
jistta keep warm"

3

yeh . . . they say
gunner never once saw'iz wife that winner 37
jus kept shovelin in that litnite
bucket atta time
was always cummin in frim th coalshed widda bucket
while th wife was goin out widda ieshes . . .

JIM LOVENZANNA

i remember sitting in jimmy hoy's place one sunday
listening to old lovenzanna and others recalling stories
about the thirties
lovenzanna spoke of the time before he moved to the village
how he and a neighbour planted crops four years straight
though nothing grew (the land slowly drifting away)
how the neighbour grew sad and spoke less each time they met
and finally lost faith in faith
no longer speaking at all in the end –
lovenzanna remembered something as though it were a dream:
i was driving past his place one day
it was cloudless and bright and very hot that day
and i saw the threshing machine going full blast
and nick sweating beside it with a huge rack load of thistles
i felt kind of funny and thought maybe i was seeing things
anyway i stopped my team and walked over to him and said
"nick – what the hell's up?"
nick's eyes looked like twin moons as he grinned and answered
"threshing jim – must be going 40 bushels to an acre
the best crop i've had in years"
lovenzanna said the mounties arrived the next day
and took nick away to weyburn –
he returned a few months later and the following year
the mounties found him driving his binder
through a dust storm (once again harvesting thistles)
when they approached him
he pulled a monkey wrench from the tool box
and began waving it at them – in the other hand he waved
a crumpled sheet of paper and shouted their way:
look godammit
i'm not crazy and i have proof i've bin to weyburn
now what the hell do you bastards have to prove you're not nuts?

another spring years later
lovenzanna said to friends drinking coffee in hoy's place:
before i die i want to harvest the biggest crop
that's ever been seen in the south country

that summer
summerfallowing on a new quarter added to his prairie empire
lovenzanna moved to another field
it was a hot july day as he made the first round
slowly falling asleep at the wheel he drove
into an abandoned root cellar in the farmyard on the field's edge
(late that night men from the village found him pinned
under the tractor
with a crumbled doorframe across his chest)

in the autumn a dozen men got together to combine the wheat
for the widow
they built a floor in the old barn for the last 5,000
of 33,000 bushels harvested

the evening mrs lovenzanna served the last supper
one farmer said:
too bad old jim ain't here to see it all in the granaries
mrs lovenzanna nodded and
a bottle of whiskey no one had noticed before
was being held next to her heart
she smiled and placed the bottle on the table – and said:
a little of something jim would have given the kids
this christmas

as a farmer finished pouring a glass for each man
they raised their glasses and said:
well – here's to old jim

POEM TO SITTING BULL AND HIS SON CROWFOOT

spill water's child
her horses ran four times
red leaf

indian summer
and poplars flare into the unimaginable
oranges reds and yellows

in the nearby willows
a pheasant's rusty cry rasps the silence
while i walk on this high hill –
sioux cemetery markers lean like signposts pointing
to distant constellations
names read like haiku:

brown eyes
held at bay
yellow leaf

wood mountain descends along heat waves to fade
where pinto horse butte begins
in the west

wounded horse
james wounded horse who taught me how to play pool
in my boyhood when we used to set pins
in vasile tonita's pool hall on friday mailnights –
once wounded horse leapt like a struck rabbit
high above a tenpin ball hurled his way
by some jester who wouldn't wait for the pins to be up
(i still remember how fear crossed his eyes
and moved me
the way his metal marker now mirroring the sun
casts my thoughts to sitting bull and a dream
where the lives of these people begin
where something in my life seems rooted here)

sitting bull
who dreamed of the possible
union of indians spanning the plains west to
the shining mountains –
i wonder if his dream floated like frosted helium
before his eyes
the day sun gleamed bright across waiting guns
while men dragged him feet-first from the tepee

while he rose to
crumple to the ground with his son
did his life really flow before the darkening light
his years in these southern hills
older than the meaning of name
and the gods i will never know
or the lying faces of men who betrayed him
giving him an ultimatum:
starve or surrender to the enemy

his was not the peace
his brothers the santees found here
a peace they said he too would finally find –
he did not share their sound sleep
beneath sweet smoke of willow bark flaked
and drawn through the pipe

he may not have had time to remember
the words he left us with at wood mountain:
the great spirit provided for both white and red men
but white man has grown powerful
and defies the gods –
is trying to undo all wakantanka has done

Mick Burrs

THE PLATFORM

The man approaches you in the chill air.
His boots creak on the planks.
Your hands are tied behind your back.

He places a white cotton hood
over your head – after knotting
the noose around your neck.

Now the air you breathe
is warm, your own. Your eyes
vanish behind this mask of snow.

Because your face cannot be seen
nothing is conveyed: your lips,
their silent prayer, the forgiveness

in what they say. But the man's breath
turns hot against your hooded head
before he steps away:

Louis Riel,
do you know me?
You cannot escape from me today.

LOUIS RIEL

Afterwards
his child takes
the hangman's noose

turns it back
into a ball of yarn
and gives away
the threads

These are
the loose ends
of the rainbow
he says

TERRITORIES

In Regina you walk the streets to work.
A bulldog hobbles forward, barks at you
then shrinks back to shadows
scratches at fleas
while a hawk circles
above the mowed earth
in the verdant valley of Qu'Appelle.
Tiny cacti cling to hillsides
bearing more than needles
to sweet dew of moon,
bitter smoke of sun.

In Regina you hear the guitar player blues,
beery tunes, honking of car horns,
leave your coat at the door, pay for answers
in twelve different keys
while moonclouds spread
over muted earth
and the serpentine river of Qu'Appelle.
You were the seeds, you were the harvest
now you wander among territories
sweet dew of moon,
bitter smoke of sun.

Barbara Sapergia

OLD WIVES LAKE

shallow salt lake ringed in boulders
small stone circles of old fires
shores thick with breeding birds   waters
choked with leeches and minnows
teeming with brine shrimp

in the sun no one
hears the old wives call
marsh birds drown their cries
raucous cranes and herons
on long thin legs
shrill prairie gulls

the lake is twenty miles long
visitors consult maps
imagine it the centre
of some tourist playground

the margins are etched in white
salt rushes and marsh grasses push
towards land   towards water

on your map it may say
"Johnstone's Lake"   imposed
by men who call forests and rivers
after one another
                              it is
not Johnstone's lake   through all
the long winters   in the fierce
summer sun   it still holds
blood of the old women
that dripped and seeped
into earth   to the lake
blood of women past
the time of lovers and birth

now the old wives are gone
flesh joined to air and land
bones bleached white
their fires have all died away

on newer maps they have put back
the old name   at night
the old wives cry out
with their strong voices   the hills
ring with their voices

DIRT HILLS MIRAGE

your land is in the Dirt Hills
they were told
your land is in the Missouri Coteau

    the hills   smoky blue &
    sharp in the clear October air
    Dumitru holds cracked leather reins
    in Luba's arms a bundle of shawls
    contains their son   sheltered
    against the cold   the
    waning sun

    the horses' feet
    rise and fall   dust
    on long silken hair
    everywhere they see
    rows of stooks
    flowing haystacks
    goldenrod in ditches

        the hills   the lost Romanian hills
        green villages carved in wood
        high meadows blooming goats
        & shaggy sheep

crystals of ice spin
through sun   bright sloughs
& coulees come dancing near

your land is dirt hills   (dirt?)
your land is in the coteau   (coteau?)

the sea
scavenger birds scream
pounding green waves
drown their village church
Pan pipe's wild torrents
stream through their skulls
the old hills
washed away

in her head is a charm
her mother gave to keep
their house safe   in his
a vision of young lambs
they bring a shepherd's flute
a shining axe   bright woven rugs
corn meal for *mamaliga*

crystals of ice shatter
the sun   dissolve the distance
sloughs shimmer   hover
above the land   the hills
grow tall   their shapes brought
impossibly near

HAYING TIME, 1953

the men are working in the shop
an old rusty boxcar dark inside
hot full of grease, junk, boards,
spare parts, nameless equipment

little breezes
raise circles of dust in the yard
shiver the caragana leaves

in the kitchen
you can hear the clock ticking
the old cookstove simmering
soup from fresh green peas
it's almost time

i look at the shop welding lights
play like bright stars you are not
supposed to look without a mask
you will go blind i look nothing
moves there is no sound not even
the sound of machines only wind
the caragana leaves are yellowing

grandma nods i run to the well
draw up a long rope & a quart sealer
i hear her calling the men
"hey – come on! dinner!" she whistles
her sweet piercing whistle
i can never figure out
how she does that

i beat uncle ben back to the house
we make the screen door slam
his face is red & seamed with
white rings from his mask
he shakes his head
"ninety above &
the goddamn tractor breaks down"
he pours water in the basin
splashes his face & cool
crystal drops hover in the air
he dries with a soft old towel
the water makes his face
look smooth & young again

i hand him the sealer
slippery with a fine chill mist
with both hands he tips it
gulping the icy liquid
sweet/sour buttery bits
his hot breath becomes
clouds in the jar

VISIT

auntie annie's house is hot
& full of light   perhaps
she needs the heat now
to warm her 80 year old bones
or maybe it's for the budgie
chirping its defiance of the winter

she has not seen me for 10 years
but her arms reach out to me

it hurts to put my body
in those kindly arms   to see
the smile i knew she would give
i could count on her smile
10 times out of 10
            she remembers
not my name but my face
my mother's face   perhaps
she takes me for my mother
grown young again

holding her small body
i remember hugging my grandmother
before she died warm & still strong
but with such a lightness
to her body   i was afraid
to hold her   afraid to let go

Martha E. Crawford

THIS IS AN OLD ROAD

Hard times built it.
Men wading swamp water made it.
Each given a slip of paper stating
        Government Relief
    one hundred pounds second grade flour
    one pound salt, ten of sugar
    six cakes of yeast
    and one tin of pork grease:
        one month's relief.
The new road runs parallel,
black-topped and smooth.
The old road remembers men, not machines.
And phantom voices of the dead builders
roll their boisterous echoes
in the wind of a Summer storm.

THE SCENT

Somewhere once before
        I stood
and breathed this scent in a green Spring.
What do I expect,
the rattling round of buggy wheels
        in the distance?
The beat of horse-shoes on a prairie road,
cement-hard from a dry season?
or the alkaline taste of prairie dust
mingled with eager kissing?
I kick the lumps of dried old horse-dung
to small bombs of dust.

R.E. Rashley

LOST REPLY

In spring a mallard
sudden in the weed-edge.

Then broken shell
and replicas
skittering into the reeds,
the slough alive with splashing.

Yesterday, silence.

Now the minute wedges
high, high,
and the heart-tearing cry.

Some shadowy inner thing
goes echoing.

And I will not go to the slough tomorrow
to stand face turned to the sky.

CHOKECHERRY PITS

The contour lines follow the old humus.
Trowel and brush work easily down
through the shallow droppings of time.
Stone grates – maybe a flake –
or is it a tool emerging?
"How can you tell!" people wonder.
Tools fit themselves into the function.
Hands and fingers, it seems, were always the same.
The brush comes out, and, suddenly, "Hey! Beads!" –
little black spheres in the ashes –
They are not beads, we discover –
chokecherry pits,
tossed or spat into the fire.

It was August, then, when this hearth was burning!
I picture chokecherries spread in the sun,
lustrous, crimson – rolled, and shifted, and sampled –
pemmican.
Suddenly I remember
pulling the branches down for someone,
watching the drops of blood
trickle through curled fingers –
With us it was jelly or wine.

I pause for a moment, cupping the charred pits
kneeling by a rekindled hearth,
a patch of chickweed spread like a white table,
wine, pemmican,
prairie sun,
wind sliding over the great erosion,
old brown river cutting a way to the sea.

Garry Raddysh

SUSPENSION BRIDGE

prairie hides its surprises
in the open – huge grey
clouds shielding a hailstorm,
the large brown land suddenly
twitching with movement
of a rabbit

still I was not prepared
for fantasy, not these pilings
on either bank of our common river
nor the rusted sagging cable,
the only remains
of a suspension bridge

suspension bridges
were for jungle movies,
slung over roaring cataracts,
swayed by tight-rope walkers
not afraid to slip
because they could
climb hand over hand to safety

damp leaves shudder
at the edge of the wheatfield –
drawn from the foliage I
slide down the bank, a naked boy
slipping in the mud
toward the ruined bridge
in the rain-pebbled river

IN LONG GRASS

in long grass I was half
a boy, arms and torso
sliding smoothly, my dark head
a small target
in long grass on the outskirts
of town I collected bottles to throw
in the river, sinking battleships
with keen beebee eyes

in long grass I searched
for arrowheads and indian
stone hammers, kicking at
stones I couldn't see
in the town office window we found
grooved hammers on sunstained boards
among oversized vegetables
grown by large russian women

in the dark town we raided back-
yard orchards and gardens, taking
only the good stuff, kicking at
round fat cabbages
in the grass finally lying
hidden, tense with joy, we
smothered the laughter evoked
by sudden lights in the window

WAYNE

the children were laughing because
children are always laughing
except for wayne
I can never remember wayne
laughing only burning,
his legs like dried corn stalks
suddenly alive and stumbling

dried corn stalks that smouldered
with little licks of flame
and wayne's mouth yelling not laughing

the children were dancing in the
autumn and in the smoke
around the burning corn stalks,
their smoky voices laughing

KEEPING SCORE

the pinball machine by the wall
lit up, flashed and buzzed
and the steel ball jumped
again and again   I watched
the numbers total and retotal
on the breasts of a painted lady

old men on their stools turned
sideways, ate sandwiches
and placed one elbow
on the counter   they watched
us from the far end of the room,
mouths dryly dropping crumbs

my friend bent over the flippers,
parted his moist lips and
readied his tense fingers
to jab   his charged eyes
followed the ricocheting ball
and the winking lady keeping score

GRANDMOTHER: THE WAITING

you wait in the garden
among white and red peonies,
a green cutworm on your shoulder

or on the steep stairs
of the root cellar
white haired and awkward
with the two jars of preserves, gifts

thinking the plot
beside your husband's grave
is too narrow

you wait in the neat-rowed
garden where you can
cultivate green shoots,
manage the black soil
with a hoe

or in my dream you lie
face-down on the stone floor
of a funeral parlour

your shrouded back
waiting for my touch

Lorna Uher

VERTICAL MAN

It is difficult to hide.

For two days
I crowd the gaps in a snow fence
a tall grey slab,
planed on one side
wrinkled and barked on the other
a wide upthrust arm
to block the snow from the steel
of the C.P.R.

But on the third day I hear the moan of the train
and see the men carrying thin sticks to build a new fence.

I flee across the summerfallow
to a granary hunched
grey and small against the wind.
I crawl inside and sleep
in the warmth of wheat smells
until morning and the whine
of the farmer's truck.

There is no place left to hide.

I stand still and bare on the prairie
but the wind flat-palmed
pushes me to the earth
silences me with dusty lips
surrounds me with tumbleweeds
and although I hear the heavy boots
I breathe with the wind,
I tremble with the earth.
They will not find me.

GRANDFATHER

you are not senile
my grandfather
you are eighty-seven and speak
with the crow's sharpness
you move slowly
your arthritic joints stiff
but your wide shadow is always
moving above/over us
will always move

now you are a mellowed man
gentle with your women
your daughters who hid
under the bed   curling their legs
from the whip of the willow lash
your wife who ran to open the gate
as you waited with your heavy team
your hands knotted in reins

I have known only
an old man with gentle hands
carving poplar whistles
from supple branches
hands circling small fingers
as I pressed against you
frightened by the barn closeness
of hooves

now in your apartment
I hold your hands
and cut the brittle nails/you shape
jagged edges with your jacknife
that sliced green branches
from planted trees

I AM A LAKE

i am a lake
patterned by your tracks
across the snow sifted
like white pollen
on an oval board

to cross me
you must flop on your belly
like a seal   drag your massive weight
up my legs   across my chest
leaving a warm wide print
of your passage

if you insist
on walking
cracking jagged wounds
on my cold skin
with each thud of your heavy boots
i will open up   swallow you
hold you in my frozen mud
till spring

my fishes will lay eggs
in the cups of your eyelids
my lakebirds will nest in the hair
of your arms and your black thighs
the tongue of my water will ripple
your chest

after the thaw
as your feet send roots
through the softening mud
your fist will float to the surface
a tight white blossom
opening to the sun

ALICE

i know a woman
who can leave her body
and from the ceiling's corner
laugh at her mound of flesh
sweating on sheets

she looks like a normal woman
her eyes do not twist
nor does saliva thread
her chin   but sometimes when
we face in conversation
i feel her warm breath
on the back of my neck
and once i saw her laughing face
mirrored in her eyes

i have asked her
to teach me
to stride beyond this bone closet
where i hang neck swelling
in the self-twisting rope
but her act is instinctive
and beyond learning
or perhaps i am afraid
and don't really want to know
this final deception

for each time   she says
she stays away a little longer

WEDDING MASQUE

Today I need a mouth.
With a thumb of Verry Cherry lipstick
I smear a fat square block
above my chin.
With a fountain pen
jaggedly I rip an opening.
I practise sounds that might please you.
"Yes. Yes. Yes."

I must also have eyes.
I draw two dark depths below my mind.
A blue wax crayon jabs in the iris.
I draw a star in each corner
to sparkle for your pleasure.

Green putty forms my perfect nose.
No nostrils are needed.
Fresh air must not enter.
With soft yellow soap I mold ear lobes,
permitting no holes to suck in sounds.
An empty white cloak will serve for a body.

I will fit in your pattern.
I will glide in your shadow.
I will reply
"I do. I do. I do."

TRAP/LINE RITUAL

you are caught

i have come just
in time

you have chewed the flesh
on your leg   the bone striped
red against the snow
spat beside you lie
frozen strips of flesh

i approach/wary
with my club
you do not bare
your teeth or growl
nor do you look
or whine for sympathy

we have met before

i pry the metal jaw

you gather the strips
of words and crawl
towards the coulee
dragging blood behind you

i set my leg in the trap

the teeth rip
through thick scars

the snow whitens
to a page

INNER SPACE

my spaces are vast
                  are blue

winds rip through my ribcage

redtails shriek in my throat

with a dry puckered mouth
the sun sucks my brain

i look small
and earthbound

                  but inside

is   the   sky

E.F. Dyck

FALL DAYS

These are large days

on the prairie

Each buffalo breath

dwarfed

hides in gusty winds

Skyscrapers

disappear in the fields

they sink

through the crested grass

as slowly as elevators

The days

swallow all measurements

even themselves

they are so large

LAMENT

I cannot bear it grandmother
that you born in number four village russia
peasant by birth by faith by pride
that you were let down rouged and curled and
oh so white/you were always quite brown
large moles graced your face

we bear you grandmother
your grandsons/to the grave/at the end
you did not believe we were grandsons

never believed that men
had landed on the moon/what would they do
up there you said

would not have believed
that your children who did not let you die
in their smart homes fell on your thin body
beating their breasts

you did not weep when we let
your husband down/*mawk dem tau* you said
(close him up) turned away on the arm
of your eldest son/my father

I cannot weep grandmother
cannot weep

TURNHILL

In the saucered plain
where ridges roll in the dust
and the hot sun crawls
over runted trees
there
stands the hill where the cattle turned.

Out of the smokey lovelies
along the gullies
where the land
plunges
wild as a pony to the river
he galloped away

Away from the lip
of the promised land
where trees smouldered
at the foot of the turning hill
and the house went down
with a slap and a splash.

Still
the land hangs
as a hawk
hunting the river-breaks.
A man-made tide washes
washes the hill where the cattle turned.

RIDE INTO THE HILLS

west into the rain   he rides
(in his yellow car)
the greasy road between two rows
of foxtails very familiar
will he slip into a ditch
no/up & down he rides
among the hills soft & round

he turns south/drives smack
into the rainbow's end at the edge
of a pink pasture the cows are green
the grass is gold & old wives lake
seen from the nipple of a hill
floating   far

he stops   gets out   looks back
rainbow's gone   looks south
the light drains from old wives
& the dark from the east sweeps
over the hills
                    jump to the car/wheel
                    around & race   anywhere
                    out of these hills

north to the highway he flees
the hills in the headlight's beam
separated by the ditch from the road
press/expel him & his yellow car
in the night & the moon bathes
the mocking hills in light

INSTRUCTOR

the quickest draw in moose jaw
is fred bsc engg
he on his hip like a pistol wears
his calculator
electronic gunslinger/he swaggers
down the hall
his hewlett-packard swings easy
in its padded vinyl holster

fred watches the eyes
as he faces his pupils down
it's the eyes/lighting
up like a switched-on
texas instrument/that
give them away/he guns
them down with a flick
of digits

James L. McLean

FIRST DECEIT

There was a time I understood things very well
eyes saw, ears heard, pigs built houses
bears ate porridge, words
were simply spoken truths
each morning I stood trembling
in the dusted sunlight
of my first grade classroom
silently mouthing
the words of the hymn
so God would not misunderstand
and take me for His gem.

GRANDFATHER

Once
he spat
that this land, my birthplace,
was cursed
unfit for human beings
and I
who had never smelt the heather
or heard the surf drums
pounding
on the shores of Skye
listened silently, only knowing
that I could not breathe
without the wind
or live the year around
without the first
clean fall of snow

He never learned
the secret of the trees
never heard their soughing descant
when they danced with wind

He never heard the thousand thousand
whispers of the plain
or sucked the thick sweet jam
of cactus seeds
or danced the pie
in knee-deep moonlit snow

I could have traded him
the tobacco juice miracle
of a grasshopper
for the time he touched a broadsword
said to have been whetted
on the Stone of Scone

or for his silvered memories
of the herring fleets
but he never would allow my sun
beneath the peak of his old tweed cap
and left his own sparse boyhood
under yellowed curling documents
in some forgotten kirk

The fields he gave to me
are filled with houses now
and I have crossed his ocean
by a single bridge
to other alien lands
but still I feel
the same fierce fire in my eyes
that flashed in his
to hear the pipes
and I shiver
at the same dark-shadowed piper
who welcomed him
who will
welcome me.

REMEMBRANCE DAY

BULLETIN NO. 039

SUBJECT:
RE: REMEMBRANCE DAY STATUTORY HOLIDAY,
NOV. 11, 1975

Employees will be permitted to observe the two minute silence at eleven o'clock, provided it does not interfere with the normal operation of the trains.

Elizabeth Brewster

THIRTY BELOW

The prairie wind sounds colder
than any wind I have ever heard.
Looking through frosted windows
I see snow whirl in the street
and think how deep
all over the country now
snow drifts
and cars are stuck
on icy roads.
A solitary man walking
wraps his face in a woollen mask,
turns his back sometimes
so as not to front
this biting, eye-smarting wind.

Suddenly I see my dead father
in an old coat too thin for him,
the tabs of his cap pulled over his ears,
on a drifted road in New Brunswick
walking with bowed head
towards home.

COLD TEA

The old woman is dying gradually
in the spare bedroom of the farmhouse.
She is waited on
by her unwilling daughter-in-law
and by an occasional grandchild
wandering into the room
between games of school or store
or blindman's buff.

On her bedside table
her black Bible rests
between a liniment bottle
and a glass of water
beginning to fill with air bubbles.

She would like to pour me
a cup of tea
but the pot on the dresser
has gone cold.

Gary Hyland

NEESH

Neesh the Indian conserved words
let us puff rollies in his shack
near his creek by the CN line
dozing in his rocker
while we struck matches and poses
that might have burned us all –
tough guy pre-adolescents who later
scrubbed brown fingers with snow.

Ten years at least he was there
and was never once outside they say,
there were stories about what he ate
and how he got his tobacco.
In winter by the east window
in summer by the west he watched us
playing on the long cinder hills
by the tracks and on and in his creek.

Often I thought about old Neesh
whether he was wise or mad,
whether a whole tribe slept in him
awaiting a sign of war or peace.
From Sleigh Hill one night I watched
his shadow rocking and smoking
till a winter fog intervened
and I couldn't even see the shack.

Between us, beneath the darkness
and the fog, was his creek and
under the ice, Neesh had said, was water
just a bit, refusing to freeze,
keeping the mud moist, and in the mud
were seeds and creatures still alive.
Beneath such layers I imagined Neesh
through whom I came to interpret us all.

THE SUN AND MRS. POMOSKI

A bright floral apron riding the waves of her skirt
Mrs. Pomoski walked her tidy garden aisles every August
proud as a grouse of all she had grown and
doing delicate things with her large soft hands.

More than the sun's her warmth made things grow
and not a tendril broke formation anywhere
not a filament of weed that wasn't worried out
before it sipped a day's worth of life.

In winter she baked buns, bread and biscuits
always giving our family a covered basketful,
globes as golden warm as her summer sun.
More than her face I remember that warmth.

CHIMERA

for Larry Saigeon

No one can understand the boy this day
how he can be both rider and ridden
the creature of a new mythology:
he scents moist earth, snorts mightily,
slaps a buttock, grabs an unseen rein
and gallops the fields stopping with a skid
on wet dirt in a stream-flanked lane.
No one can understand how he can be
both dam and river, motionless mover:
he steps into a stream and stands entranced
to feel around his hooves the fast cool swirl,
then sights two rustlers, draws and shoots.
It is April and there is no school
and he's half stallion in rubber boots.

COAL DAYS

$17.50 would fill the old barn's bin
with one ton of bituminous
never enough till they could charge the next
so Ed's mother took him prospecting
for what God dropped in the public domain
between the CN tracks and the sheds
where the men unloaded the trains.

Still there was the shame of scrounging
so they went out late at night
with doubled shopping bags and flashlights
a furtive housewife and her son
fingering the snow for glossy nuggets
lugging the bags a block across a field
trying to look casual beneath the streetlight
before the alley's dark relief.

His mother told him it wasn't stealing
but on the trek home he always heard sirens.

MRS. R. WAITS FOR THE BUS

Her face is a war zone:
sunglasses camouflage
eye-deep death traps,
rouge of the wounded
stains the cratered cheeks,
two straight trenches
slash from nose-ridge
to mouth edge
as if the kerchief
caught sags of skin
in its cruel twist,
with a small snarl
the mouth emplacement
covers the salient chin.
She opens her purse
with a musicbox click
and I hear men marching
to martial strains.
The bus is late.
There may be bloodshed.

HE PLAYED GOLF

He played golf
collected cups from tournaments
& sports page accolades
taught wobbly women
    left arm straight
    right elbow tight
so they could talk
18 holes a week

Winters
he clerked
or drove a truck
or was unemployed
or mopped someone's office
where every hall
was a fairway
every carpet
a green

Summers
were a carnival
of silver shafts
slicing sunlight
into winning scores
till the tendons tightened
his hands into claws
too stiff
to grasp the clubs

Now in spring he brings them out
to polish & practise
a stroke or two
the hands clumsy as crabs
along the leather grips

David Waltner-Toews

TANTE TINA'S LAMENT

Hänschen is a fool
and I am his mother,
Lord forgive us both.
Hänschen struts about the city
like a chicken.
He wears a pink shirt
and plaid, big-bottomed hosen.
When he was little,
his bottom was like a zwieback.
I spanked his little buns
and how he crowed!

Now he wags his tongue at me
and thinks I am ignorant.
He says farmers have no brains
they should all be businessmen.
He says farm girls don't know how to walk
and I don't know how to barbecue a steak.
Oh his heart is full of borscht
and his words are sour.
Don't call me Hänschen, he says.
My name is John.
Do I not know my son's name?
Did I not argue for six nights
with David, my husband, about that name?

On Wednesday night
the young people go to church.
They eat platz and give testimonies.
The girls have long golden hair.
Their cheeks are rosy from harvest
and dresses cover their knees.
When the young people sing together
it is heaven above and earth below
with sopranos and basses.

But my Hänschen
goes to dance in the city.
He has a girl friend.
She smears grease on her lips.
Her blond hair is cut and curled
and her knees are bare
like a young calf.
When they dance
their legs are noodles
and the music is a tractor.
The girl friend says it is not a shame
for a woman to cut her hair.
She thinks Mennonites are like Hutterites
and has never heard of roll kuchen.
What good can come of that?

Hänschen says she is a modern girl.
He says we must speak English to her
because she goes to the United Church.
He says Low German is a pile of manure.
Listen here, my little boy.
I will surround you with Low German.
I will speak piles of it to you.
Then you will know what Low German is!
Then you will remember –
a mother's anger is a willow switch.

He does not listen.
We are poor, he says.
We do not know how to make money.
He wants to be rich, like the English,
and save us all from Mannagruetze.
His heart is tight as a peppernut.
His head is a piroshki
stuffed with fruit.

In the barn, the cats eat mice
and wait for milking time.
When my man comes in
I serve him dinner, steaming on a plate.
But my son does not know happiness.

On New Year's Eve
we go to church at night,
and on Easter
as the sun rises
we sing praises.
Hänschen is at church by eleven
on Easter.
On New Year's Eve
he goes to dance.
He does not even come to hear the children
on Christmas Eve!
When he was still wet behind the ears
he was a wise man in the play.

Oh my son
my heart is heavy,
thick as glums.
If you come home
it will rise, light and sweet.
I will make you porzelky for breakfast
and we will celebrate the New Year
every morning.

TAKE-HOME EXAM

The mind is faster than the womb.
Three months after we, for one night only,
tested fate, the child is testing us,
and our sterility is no longer the question.
At six a.m. I find him, or her –
the *kid* for Pete's sake –
lying between us on the bed,
asking questions.
What makes you think you'll be such a good father?
I don't have to answer.
This exam wasn't scheduled.
I at least want my breakfast first.
What about overpopulation?
Don't you care about starving people?
I roll over: O.K., so I'll skip breakfast.
At the table
the little unborn being
jostles for the space between us,
crowding up the silence
where we once held hands,
handing out questionnaires like a psychologist.
Who'll take care of me?
Are you both going to work?
Or just the father?
Will you be sexist role models?
As we flee on our bicycles
the voice calls down the street:
How do you expect me to turn out
if you don't spend any time with me?
Later, seeing you in your swimming suit,
I'd swear you weren't even showing.

OLD FRIEND

A lunch bucket is an old,
bald-headed friend.
In the morning
he goes to work with you.
He sits on the car seat beside you
not saying much.
After you punch in
you have to find a place for him to wait.
The Company thinks of him
as a fifty year man, now retired.
They're not sure he's welcome.
They only let you talk to him
at ten, and twelve, and three
and, even then, they whistle over your shoulder,
"Visiting hours are almost over."
You talk about sandwiches.
He yarns out a long thermos of coffee.
Sometimes, at ten or three
he tells plum jokes;
the words burst in your ear
and the juice runs down your chin.
He'll even go on the picket line with you.
Right beside the RCMP man
he'll open his big mouth.
"It's a piece of cake," he says.
Driving home with you at four-thirty
he's feeling kind of tired and hungry.
He'll probably yawn
right through the football game.

Dennis Gruending

UNCLE JIM AND THE HORSES

Old Jim (six foot five) wears 10 gallon hats
smokes big cigars and walks the narrow
streets of Bruno
                    a weathered stallion rearing
straight as a singletree at 89
Jim measures his life in horses

Born 1888: Dad was drivin a team of greys then. Best damn horses in the county.

Emigrated 1905: I was workin a livery barn in Minnesota. Told my brother I was comin up here. Got off the train in Rosthern, took a job breakin horses for the fella what owned the livery barn.

Homesteaded 1906: Never was much at farmin. Took to trailin broncs. Picked em up from ranchers in Alberta, broke em, trailed em back 500 miles to sell to farmers.

Married 1917: I'd ben goin with Annie for 11 years I think it was. Told er not to wait. But a good woman's like a good horse: wait at that hitchin rail forever and a day.

Trading: There was money in horses. I was still tradin in 65. Shipped a carload down to a fella in North Dakota. Think they kilt em for glue. I'd still be tradin but I can't see nothin.

Indians: I got nothin against em. Hell I slept with em on the trail. Ate their food. Didn't trade too many horses with em though. Had them spotty ponies. Nobody wanted em.

Gambling: Had an old crow once. Run acrost a fella lookin for a trade. At night durin a poker game in Humboldt. Fella said his horse didn't look too good. I said hell I'll trade even. Next morning I saw that horse. Like the fella said she didn't look too good. She was stone blind.

SHOE JOHN

made shoes at his window
by the light from the snow
on the street

in the town lived alone
in the back of a shack
by the pool hall

at dusk in the hall
played pool with them all
eyes red from the smoke
in the room

black night
chest pain like a vice
pulled himself across the ice
green bills in a bag
talked once of his wife
died

Shoe John
Good John
Shoe John

Geoffrey Ursell

THE OLD MEN IN SPRING

the old men have emerged once more
into the spring & armed with axes
& shovels they gather, lining the
streets, & make careful motions of
chopping and lifting, clearing the
ice from the paths, turning small
pools into trickles & then into
streams in the gutters. once more
the old men have emerged & attend to
the rebirth of spring, easing the grass
of the chill & the weight, & watching
the softening earth. they suck the
warm air & the sun into their wintery
bodies, watching the flow & thinking
of gardens, the moist clods of earth
turning heavy on spades, row after row
to the end, as once more the old men
have emerged to be warmed, as they lean
on wood handles worn smooth with their
work, & closing their eyes, rest foreheads
on hands, & remember their friends
in the earth.

FARMYARD

the house is split
in two: founded on
stone, rising wood
above: held within
a shelter-belt of
poplars, seedlings
set into the earth
50 years ago (some
now overthrown   naked
roots brittling in
the fervent air)

behind the house, between
the garden & the trees, a
rounded, plank-wood cover
rests on circled stones

i lift the rim & dip
eyes full of dark   &

a brown & scarlet lizard blinks
its amber lids, loses hold,
drops down to
                              there is
no sound   (there is
no sound)
              of water

                              the well
is dry & slowly filling now
with things that will not work,
that have worn out, appliances
and parts of old machines – a
seeder, ice-box, kitchen-range
that swallowed wood

i drop a
pebble, listen for the sharp
metallic note to sound & echo
round the dripping rust, the
moss, the silent ring of stone

WE BURN THE SUN

i cut the kindling for the fire,
choosing wood without knots to
impale upon a careful quarter-
swing before plunging it upon the
earth below in splitting blows

in the fireplace i crumble news-
papers, smudged with old deaths
and things for sale, then i lay
the wood upon its brother

the
match, touched at several points,
ignites a quick and growing flame
that reaches up and around the wood
and lingers over it. the wood is slow
to catch, but finally the kindling
heat is reached and the blaze leaps
for the open chimney, sucking in the
air we breathe for its own combustion

this is not our evening's entertainment

the fire crackles and spits sharp coals
against the dark protective screen.
i read or play guitar, occasionally i
add a piece of wood

we do not pay enough
attention to the fire. we burn the growth
and rest of years. we burn the touch of
moon and stars. we burn the rise of sap
and fall of leaves, the scent of pollen
and the snow-bent twig. we burn the flight
and quick caress of birds, the trace of
crawling worms and bugs. we burn the sound
of wind in boughs. we burn the sun

we

burn them all to flickering coals
upon the grate at night, to soft grey ash
beneath cold iron in the slant of early
morning light

&TOUCH

at 3 a m you
run on the spot
for 15 minutes
in the bathroom

(i imagine your bare feet
touching, leaving, touching
the cool little tiles
on the floor)

and i hear
the slowing patter
here in bed

you stop,
you open the door,
turn off the light,
you are coming to
our room

i almost feel
the radiance
of your hidden
nakedness, &

sense your shape
move near
our bed, &

reaching out for love
i meet your warmth
&touch
your bending head

Robert Currie

THE RIDE

The boy squatted on the bank
his knees gawking from ragged pants
as they slid around the bend
   Want a ride kid? Hop on
He leapt for the raft
skidding on the slippery wood
but a hand held him from the water
and dropped him on an apple box
   Sit there
They pushed through the bulrushes
and poled toward the bridge
   Okay kid   On top a that beam
   There's a pigeon nest   You get it
The boy knew enough not to argue
Where the river slapped the pilings
green with slime
there was a cross-piece
running at an angle
and he took it slowly upward
Groping on the beam
he felt pigeon droppings
then the nest
two eggs warm on his palm
   Anything in it?
He shook his head and started down
   Get yer ass back up there
And there were claws tightening on his neck
   Now toss us the nest
He paused looking around
And there was nothing he could do
but drop the nest
watch the broken yolk of his lie
spread across the raft
   Ya like them pigeons so much
   ya can stay with em

Their laughter floated back to him
as the raft drifted downriver
leaving him to wait
arms wrapped around a timber
wood rough against his cheek
Above   a pigeon
circling in the empty sky

THE DIVER

The bridge like a Roman fort
held the river and the beach
held our vision steady through waving heat
held us all while the solitary figure
struggled up the arch
his knees braced against the rivets
Below someone shook out his towel
while others bet upon his chance
At the summit of the span he rose
his arms outstretched
flung a cross against the sun
and the whole world hung beneath him
our eyes nailing him to the sky
Suspension for an instant and forever
A slow plunge toward the water
and he came down from above
dropping beneath the surface like a stone
The river circling away
grew silent as held breath
                    still as death
Then from unknown depths
his head broke the water
shook out a crown of sunlit spray
brought release   new life
thrilling in our chests

GETTING IT ON

This is Sam the Man Spenser again
back for another 55 fantastic minutes
While the news was on ladies and laddies
I had one sick fella on the phone
Wanted me to play that John R. Cash song
How high's the water Momma?
Five feet high and risin
With the crest still to hit River Park
we'll have none of that   No siree
It's golden oldies all weekend
the best of early fifties rock
taking you back to where it all began
But first a public-service message
on behalf of the guys at EMO
Puh-lease stay off the telephones
at least whenever possible
Our man at Sask. Tel.
reports lines burning up
They can hardly handle the load
Guess everybody's phoning
to see how high the water is
So you take it to heart
out there in radio land
Now let's get it on again
with the hot songs from the cool fifties
If you've got a favourite
give us a call right here
at the key to the world's breadbasket
CKCB in Moose Jaw

RAILROAD MAN

I lika de trains, he says.
I uze ta vork on de saction geng.
He remembers it
those first blisters of distant days
the heave of the sledge hammer
with the sweat running
and the long hours pumped into sundown
on the shaft of the handcar.
What he'd liked
was his noon dream
with grasses stirring easy in the breeze
sun warm on the lunch pail
the rails singing for his flattened ear
and for the sweeping train
that set wild grasses bucking
and tumbled his mind from sunburn and callous.
For a moment then he would ride
crisp and white in the dining car
silent with its courtesy of waiters
his destination in the glamour
where the twin rails meet.
And when the grasses ceased tossing their manes
he always tapped his thin wallet,
nodding his head.
Now he kicks the cinders
and slaps his bulging hip.
I lika de trains, he says.
But dey don't go nowhere much no more.

PHOTOS IN THE FRASER CANYON

Against the hard face of the mountain
a hard man
his face cupped in his hand
his thoughts blasting granite.
Beneath him a sheer cliff
that drops like a guillotine
into the Fraser's slaughterpen.
His eyes strip away the quartz
where the C.P.R. must go.
        Andrew Onderdonk
he had the government contract
and he would do the job.

In a later picture the same scene
still etched in sepia
but now the mountain is torn by tunnel
the cliff face scarred by rail and trestle.

Front and centre the excursion train
passengers in frozen smiles for the photograph
that does not reach down the line
to the labourers' camps huddled in snow,
that does not show the unmarked graves
of Chinese coolies half a world away
from Kwang Tung province and home.
        Andrew Onderdonk
he had the government contract
and he had done the job.

INTIMATIONS

Striving to make them sense
their own mortality
I gripped the shrunken head,
a rubber toy but grisly,
addressed it as Yorick,
and no gorge rose.
But after class
one boy shied towards me:
"I was just wonderin if . . . well . . .
Howdja like a real skull for that part?"
Trying not to think
of what was left headless
I seized upon his offer.
Now when Hamlet holds
the jester's skull,
the classroom grows
quiet as the grave.
They see the end,
and cannot laugh at that.

MORNING RIDE

Six in the morning
and dark outside
Wind already blowing
as I drive you to the airport
In places snow
building again where a blade
has channeled out the road
Open spots and ground drift
pulling the car toward the ditch
Before the overpass
we ease around a semi
jack-knifed across the road
and fishtail for Regina and the plane
that will lift you from the prairie

In the half-light paw marks
appear from nowhere in the ditch
move like ghosts beside us
until we see the mongrel
whiter than snow
running with us at the east
to chase the day into the sky
It leaps a snowdrift
   rises with the vaulting sun
The whole prairie a sudden radiance

Glen Sorestad

STOTSKI'S POOLROOM

Outside Stotski's poolroom under October blue
the old men of the village sit on rough benches
soak the waning warmth of the autumn sun
and dream of past harvests heavy stooks
of hard wheat waiting for the threshing machine

Inside Stotski's poolroom pale young men move
in the dim room where shaded lights focus
on the smooth green fields of faultless felt
and snooker balls make snicking sounds
like hazel nuts dropped by red squirrels
as they stockpile against the coming cold

THE WINDSOR HOTEL, BUCHANAN

Two farmers sit at separate tables
                    in silence
their backs to one another
the only patrons of the moment.

The question of an irrigation ditch
                    divides them
and has for ten silent years
of back-to-back neglect.

Their harvests – grain and children
                    grown and gone
wheat and barley, sons and daughters
grown and gone, east and west.

Soon they will have each other only
and the endless empty silence between them.

BEER AT COCHIN

The lazy August fire
wanted quenching.
Even the slightest breeze
from the lake
could not suppress the knowledge
that Cochin pub was near
and cool
and wet.

Entering the dim-cool (alive
with beer promises) room
is so good you want to stop
forever
the moment
to hang suspended.

The Indians and Metis have their own
section in the pub at Cochin –
no cordons
no signs
no markers
of any kind
no nothing so blatant
but in Cochin
they know where to sit.
Everyone in the room knows
even you
total stranger
even you know too.

But you ignore it and sit down
next to a table of Indians
and wait
and it doesn't take long
no
not long at all.

Someone flips a switch
and conversation
in the room is silenced
and even the table next to you
is frozen.
And the bartender comes over
his face pained
suggesting a recent family death
and he asks
if you wouldn't like to
move closer to the bar
and you are well aware that
it really isn't a question
now
or ever.

WIND SONGS 11

(for bob w.)

the red fox
we have set to flight
is a flash fire
against
the dying gold
of the wheat stubble

a short moment
and we are not certain
there ever was
a burning motion
in the fading fall
light
that closes now
around us

James A. MacNeill

CIGARETTES AT A FOWL SUPPER

We sat around the table
In the church basement
And he afraid to smoke
Although his need was greater than mine
Should we ask the minister
He said   I said
Go ahead   he said
He's too far away
I'd have to shout
Do you really think he'd mind
I said   no   and then I said
I didn't think
He'd mind   but find out
Anyway   That's the trouble
With questions of religion and philosophy –
Everybody's afraid to ask
Huh!   he said
We'd better go outside.

Audrey Johannessohn

GOOD MORNING, LLOYDMINSTER

Box elder branches and poplar
Scroll work on a raging dawn
Day demanding its right of birth
Night and the half light grudgingly
Move over the opposite sky.

Sleepy eyes, blue jeans and bitter sweet coffee
They crowd the truck-stop cafes
Oil trucks and cattle liners like dogs
Following each other nose to tail
Down highway sixteen.

Old farmers walk the meridian street
The Prairie's history is written
In the lines of their faces
The morning air is incensed
With crude oil and manure.

Stephen Scriver

IN SHAPE

just to move, man
feel those muscles stir again
long summer of beer and sun

just to move
hear the old heart pounding
full of one more season
feel the body burst again
charged with easy sweat

two weeks of up, down
                        up, down
                        backwards, forwards
blow that whistle, man
sounds like music now it's easy

. . . move, man
only six strides down now
blue/white /red/white/blue/white
around the net
leg over leg
and blue/white/red

lungs smooth with swelling breath
legs pump   push that ice again

ah, but just to move

THE SLAP SHOT

(for Rudy Wiebe)

You see, the problem is:

to get your head above and
just ahead of the puck

to slide your forehand down
the shaft of your stick as you
pull it back

and with your back leg leaving
the ice just before your stick
hits

striking the ice just a few
inches behind the puck

hitting it about the
middle of the blade

while aiming at the corner
of the net

and if you have to think about
that, brother,

it just isn't there

Don Kerr

FRED, IT'S STILL ALL RIGHT

I

people who are themselves
on the near side to death
meet again at mama's funeral
the light in the room
is a five o'clock winter light
where they go for a drink
to talk

"Mama told me,
the night I was born . . . "
"Now look, fred, I'm going to
tell you something you don't
know about yourself . . . "
life is still there
every sentence turns over years
there's some pain
but they are on their feet
tense for the next moment

he says (she doesn't hear)
tomorrow I can mow the grass
with the power mower
and so keep the world in order

she says (he doesn't hear)
today I can polish mama's silver
for company as if tonight
were something special
laughter wouldn't die

II

in mama's garden
remember hiding in the peas
and the buzz of the sun
and how the wood fence
crawled with little bugs
we sat and shelled peas
and hucked them at
jane on the swing

who apparently swung off to the states
with charlie and his model t
she died   the fist of the sun
pounded her down
"she always wore such pretty
white pleat skirts"

there's always a nice minute
at the edge of a hurt
the smell of the fridge
a sandwich with mayonnaise
and beef and pickles in it
"fred,
I'm happy the sun's out today"

STANDARD TRUSTS NO. 2

It was at the end an awful stomachful of mess
and the dust the cats kicked up was some of it
seventy years old and stunk
That was the smell of defeat of all the farmers,
mortgage foreclosed
by Standard Trusts (some standard, some trust)

If justice were the criterion
for buildings to live
what would we leave?
the library maybe
and a terrace house where an absentee landlord
forgot to raise the rent

The Mayor says tear em all down
and build a new white city
and he cuts ribbons with a flourish
for Marathon and Trizec

What the hell,
on a nice day everything looks good,
lay on enough sun
even the Mayor looks like an historic monument.

Ken Mitchell

THE WITCH

The witch traversed our neighbourhood
at least three times a week
uttering crazy curses at our upright lives.
She tramped her warlock hordes
in strict formation
through the pansy beds in Gerlachs' yard
to the back alley, across several rows
of Mr. Birley's Sweet Bantam corn,
past Kingsway Clover Farm store
to the soccer field at Saint Joe's School.

There she called her legions to a halt,
her long white hair whipping in the wind
while we snickered in the weedy ditches.
She would raise her sunbright sword
(a strip of chrome
from a '48 Ford hammered to a cross)
and harangue her invisible minions
in a wild jabbering whinny
that turned our brains to slush,
jabbing her bright blade at the ranks
of green-trimmed houses in our street.

And one time at us five
crouched chortling in the pigweed.
Corbett Elstrom, our hero and bully,
leaped up and pitched a stone,
while we flattened the weeds laughing
at her furious yammering retreat.
But within a month Corbett met a train
on the high-level C.N.R. trestle
and though we followed his
slow spinning
flight to the river
with great attention
never found him
for the funeral.

LOFT

The old grey barn my father built
is burning down
under a column of oily smoke,
releasing all the delicious seizures
our hearts felt in the hay loft
when we plunged like stricken swans
to the prickly billows of sweet alfalfa.

The ruined bunkers of our mock wars
lie buried under this monument
of black smoke: the pyramid bales,
the long labyrinth tunnels
of wheat straw bleached to silver
are crumbling into slag.

The rough cough of pine timbers
popping their knots in fiery rage
silences the eerie echoes of Tarzan yells
that swung in long looping yodels at the end
of my father's lariat tied to the beam
of the black-hipped roof, my brothers
and cousins flashing out and in
among the flares of dusty sunshine
sifting down from the cupolas.

As it burns, we cry at the loss.
Not of the barn, because next month
my father will cart a new one in
on timbers chained to a dozen wheels,
hauled by a Mack truck. No.

But the loss of days
we laid on the tops of breathing stacks
of oat straw, hearing the pigs munch
orange rinds on the floor below,
gazing at the squared rafters
where Bluebar pigeons muttered, unaware
of the angry flames which threatened
their airy sanctuary.

Luetta Trehas

THROUGH THE GARDEN GATE

The child flitted through the evening, through the garden gate,
to the blue cabbage with its weight
of large smooth flowers of wet-cool leather-silk.
Here she might find a rabbit with silver fur
sprinkled over with nutmegs,
and it would skip, all legs
and ears and thistledown.
But instead a brown bird stirred beneath the plants
sleepy-flying, loose-winged
fanning the rattling petals of the cabbage.
And the child cried out her sharp delight
her heart floating in fantasy
as she chased the bird, running faster than breath –
like a butterfly veering sidewise:
to catch the bird-wings, the feather-breast
and hold them in her arms and make a nest.
Oh! she would cradle-doll the drowsy bird!
but the sky got darker, lower,
lower, darker-blurred
and she heard
her name calling itself through the garden gate.

Ronald Marken

BIRD WORD

A sparrow treads his small mate from the sky.
My daughter's year-bright eyes absorb the bird;
Her fingers, lips define him, shape the word:
"Bir! Bir!" All feathers flash at her sharp cry.
She says no different though for bat, or fly,
Or bathroom paper swan; all wings "Bir"-stirred,
One common flock, undesignated, blurred,
Bat, fly, and sparrow proffer no reply.

Her saying changes nothing. Sparrows mate,
And flies breed blue-bummed millions in spring.
I name whole garden plots of flowers amiss;
They flower still. What's the specific weight
Of word play anyway? Is "Bir" a thing?
My daughter thinks it is. She thinks. It is.

Barry Stevens

THE LOVE OF MUD

Mud loves children;
See, on this dreary day
How it hugs, holds hands,
Dances with them.

It is not right to say
The children are to blame
For bringing mud inside:
Mud loves children.

When they leave,
Mud would go on dancing,
Hugging, holding hands,
And follows the children in.

Do not blame the children:
Try to understand
The love of mud,
How it hugs.

GRADE FIVE GEOGRAPHY LESSON

Children never get to the point,
They surround it.
The importance of the point
Is the landscape of it.
You begin by discussing
"The Rainfall of Vancouver Island"
And somebody has an uncle who lives there.
And there is an uncle in Alberta
Who has a zillion cows,
Some chickens and a horse
(We get to feed the chickens
And ride the horse),
Which brings us to an uncle
In Saskatchewan, who has a house where
Deer pass the kitchen window
Every morning (He takes us out
And shows us where they go).
If there were no uncles on Vancouver Island
It would never rain there.

Anne Szumigalski

THE WEATHER

You are reading to me

You spread the newspaper out
across your knees
It crackles dully as you fold back the pages

Your heavy thumbs
pressing along the creases
leave a grey smear

PLANE DOWN ON THE BARRENS
you read

BOY TORN BY HUSKIES

TWO PERISH IN BLIZZARD

your voice is warm and exultant

I have been dead all winter
no one has noticed it

my bones, sewed up in a cheerful
print sack, balanced on the seat of a chair
answer all your questions
my skull nods
I creak as I bow from the waist
agreeing – always agreeing

I shuffle into the kitchen to make tea
soft dust rises from the floor
I pour and pour

the cups remain empty

IT WASN'T A MAJOR OPERATION

the surgeon joined us
with a long wire he threaded
through your left earhole
and into my right one

when we woke up from the anesthetic
we had to begin practicing at once
every time you nodded your head
I inclined mine
we bobbed together this way and that

when the wire was too taut
there was a knotted feeling in my head
when it was too slack
it looped and caught in my necklace

but now we have got used to
the continual lolling motion
and are able to go
for a short walk every day

this morning while we were
admiring the lilies
a row of birds sat down on our wire

night has fallen now
and they are still here
nine sparrows and a kingbird

NETTLES

When I am old
I will totter along broken pavements
the strings of my boots undone
smelling a bit strong like any
fat old woman who has forgotten
which day is Tuesday
(my bath night if you like)

stiff my clothes from old dirt
not sweat at my age mumbling
the cracked enamel mug

eleven cats playing
in my weedy yard drinking
my little ration of milk
with me   and withy withy
the cats circle around my house
at night singly filing
in and sleeping on the
saggy stained bed and the chair
and the crumby tabletop

One day they will find me dead
O dead dead
A stinking old bundle of
                                        dead
and in my hand
a peeled wand

and in my ear a cricket sitting
telling me stories and predictions

and the time of night

LONG DISTANCE

My wife left me
When we were both quite young
She said she was going to visit her cousin
There must have been more to it than that

Last summer she came back
Just before harvest
I awoke and she was there
Baking pies in our wedding dishes

She's a grey and folded woman now
Even her lips are creased
But sometimes when she sits there phoning
A curve of her cheek or arm
Reminds me of the girl she once was

What good is that to me?
I want to remember her always
As she is now

A CELEBRATION

Our grandmother had gout
(I think it was that)
there were chalk deposits on her knuckles
that stuck right through the skin
she used to amuse us children
by drawing five simultaneous lines
on the blackboard with the back of her hand
it must have been painful

last summer she died

she was drowned in the sea on her birthday
while swimming off Portland Head
it was a cool and windy day
but nothing would keep her
from the stormy water

they buried her on the southdowns
under a hummock of grass

But those limey spikes
grew rapidly in that soil
they branched underground
like the twigs of a great tree
they grew upwards from her desiccating hands

by September they poked out at the surface
a wide circle of little chalky stubs
I think they might have leafed out amongst the short grass
but autumn is a poor time for sprouting

when All Souls' came we lighted
eighty of them for holy candles
they burned brightly for a while
and then they wrinkled and browned
and flickered out

next year they may flower with rockroses
or stiff honeycomb corals

that's one of the reasons
we are waiting and hoping for the spring

GREY-EYED FRANCES

People are always asking me:
"Do you have children?"
"Is your mother still living?"

What they mean is:
"Have you a husband?"
"Are you alone in your bed?"

I have had this photograph taken
of my mother and myself
my daughter
and her daughter

we three women are smiling
but the child is gravely staring
out of her dark corner
over the drooping posy
of washed-out cloth violets
she is holding

small Frances
grey-eyed Frances
she is sometimes spiteful
always forgiving

I am wrapping the picture
to send to an old lover of mine
someone I haven't heard from
in ten years

I am doing it out of spite
it has nothing to do with love

UNTITLED

"I think of my poems as trees"
said the self-conscious poet
who liked to talk about his work
he made a great impression at parties
and once on TV when he was interviewed
by the farm correspondent
of a national magazine

he wanted to say that he thought
of his work as a field of wheat
but how could he explain the harvest
when the wheat is cut
and the ears combined out?

One night a poem did grow
in him like a tree
it grew in the dark   he awoke
impaled on its trunk
all his entrails were wood
and his toenails had taken root
ah, now he had to stand still

the bones of his fingers became twigs
that scratched at the inside of his flesh
"write" they commanded
"spring is here"

and he could feel how the whole tree
despised him
and hated him for not becoming
its glory of leaves

Mark Abley

SCRIMSHAWS

For weeks my hands have shone and ached
with bone, rock, art

Now the palm of my right hand is ivory
hacked from the mouth of a sperm whale:
the image engraved there, staring at me,
was made by a whaler in the last century

Deep in the mother ship, for weeks he carved:
the ocean had heaved with mammals,
their wasted blood had stained its water scarlet:
he crouched, painstaking, the stone-hard hands
clutching a jack-knife, incising
on the huge dead tooth
harshly the deaths of beasts and the swarm
of men, boats, weapons

Each time I look, the lines deepen:
the stripes of my flesh stand etched in black,
the lifeline is the surface of a fatal sea:
any survivors held their breath
in the lightless depths of its jaw

But the winding palm of my other hand
was a gift from sea to land:
a nautilus which the sailor gathered
in Fiji, combing the wrack of a beach

He poised a sailing needle to the shell
for weeks in the dim cabin,
struggling to engrave in his mind the face
of a farm girl he'd known in Kentucky:
then he cut into the mother-of--pearl
the coils and lines that had formed her,
framing her neck and swirling head
with goldenrod, bluegrass and roses:
the plants of the continent wreathe her slim face

This beauty wounds and tugs:
no matter what I reach for, what I try to hold,
images get in the way,
brighter the older I grow

Sometimes I wake before dawn,
the waves in my body throbbing:
fingers of shell and fingers of tooth
clasp needle and knife, both mine
till the sun washes a salt ocean of light
over the brittle land

FARMING THE MOUNTAIN

The soil is stoned, reluctant,
but you say you love the meagre air
and the bruised pines. At marmot height
dark bushes smell of gin: the rocks stand
implacable. With a smile
your crowned silver tooth would flash
like a jewel long buried in the cramped earth;
but your face is drawn as a miner's.

Evening arrives on time: *let's go*
into the fields. The implements
wait in their shed. They came with you up
from one of the dank valleys,
rifted with fern and poplar, you found
so hard to stand. The plucked sunset
lasts five minutes,
feathering my urban hands with light.

It's time for the news:
no hijacks of the sun: *let's go*
into the fields. Nothing can halt
the stunted evergreens lapsing grey,
the world itself growing tenuous. Our words
scud ahead of their bodies, bodies
weary as the farmed, drained earth.
And now, as the tufts of saxifrage rise
away from your own plants, now
the desperation of high places.

Shall we have a quiet night?
These pale accusing eyes
of pebbles occupy the scrag among lean,
straggled stalks of corn. Their jagged
night vision strokes our feet.
A perfect end?
The twilight's dead. *Let's go*
into the fields.

Ralph Ring

where your mountains meet
my plains do our movements
touch do our words
our eyes all aching
with meaningless voice become nothing
but near miss
each time we venture into forbidden
past

we have chosen to meet   here
i coming slowly out of skywind&grass
you inching smiling coming down
from your rock hulks that cut
sky   block the sun
about your waist a careful vial
of mountain water
your fingers twist
around a piece of polished shale
strung & sweaty about your neck

i offer you a prairie crocus
and seeds for more   i offer you
the sky
you laugh say you
want a section of soil
to plant your fir your mountain ash
say you have never enjoyed
sunsets

and so tonight we will
sleep together neither one
accustomed to foothills
                to foreign soil

for hours i will lie awake
tracing with my fingers your back
with my eyes   your rock
looming grey
                                        & waiting

come morning   you will climb
a rocktip close
to the sun
                    watch a body fade
into prairie sky   hear words
silenced in seedsong
washed into wind

Nancy Senior

ST. GEORGE

My dragon always loved walks
He used to go to the wall
where the golden chain hung
and take it in his mouth
laying his head on my lap
sideways, so the fire wouldn't burn my skirt

He looked so funny that way
with his wings dragging the floor
and his rear end high up
because he couldn't bend his hind legs

With him on the leash, I could go anywhere
No band of robbers dared attack

This morning in the woods
we had stopped for a drink
where a spring gushes out of a cave

when suddenly, a man in armour
riding a white horse
leapt out of the bushes
crying "Have no fear
I will save you"

And before I could say a word
he had stabbed my dragon in the throat
and leaping down from the horse
cut off his head
and held it up for me to see
the poor eyes still surprised
and mine filling with tears
He hadn't even had time to put out his claws

And the man said
"Don't cry, Maiden
You are safe now
But let me give you some good advice

Don't ever walk alone in the woods
for the next time you meet a dragon
there might not be a knight around to save you"

Under the paved surface
inhabited by cars
trucks
motor bikes
snowmobiles
and power boats

special light effects
on the plastic water lilies
are explained by the guide

This alternation of bright and weaker light
produced by the rotation of a filter
with irregular perforations

shows how, in olden days
you could see light and shadow
passing in turn
over the surface of the water

The bright light was from the sun
and the weaker light
was caused by clouds
passing between it and the earth

When you looked up
you could see them
like balls of fluffy nylon

If you will just look up now
at the ceiling
you can see these white clouds
projected against a background of blue
as the sky appeared in those days
to the naked eye

Last night I learned to fly
Oh, nothing spectacular
no leaping over tall buildings
at a single bound
I just rose
a couple of feet from the ground
and moved around in the air

Very handy
for crossing wet floors

I kept trying it out again
until my roommate's boy friend
said I was getting boring
So I stopped flying
around him

(If he could fly
he'd expect his picture in the paper)

I thought of doing it
the first day of class
to impress the students

But if it depended on mood
and I were tense
It might not work

And nothing is less impressive
than a teacher
standing in front of the room
flapping her arms

Byrna Barclay

NOTHING SO FINAL

You/like Poundmaker
allow women
to speak in-council
sometimes

You say I am free to go
but I am held down
by your words
stretched
in four directions

With you
there is no word
for goodbye
so you devise
other separations
tell me   your other love
will be a sister to me
but plan to trade me
for a horse
                    give me
to your friend

You say I am free
with other buffalo-
running mares
then tie me
to an anchor-post
sleep
with the other end
of the rope
in your hand

Terrence Heath

Your fingers and hands,
Coated in garden loam,
Black, caked.
Softness,
Kept soft by hand lotion,
Soft to caress.
The cold May wind
Reddens your wrists
Makes your nose run
Tangles and mats your hair

If I kept a journal, I'd say:
    Today she was beautiful
And if I kept a diary, I'd say:
    Today I was beautiful

Today I am cold;
Twice already I have
shuddered
as if a chilling wind
abraded my skin.
My mother would have said:
"Someone is walking on your grave"
I am just tired,
depressed.
Her adage: "Live today,
as if you were going to die tomorrow"
flows over me
like the currents
of an unmoving lake.
I lie here in the cold shallows
moving my fingers wearily
wondering if I would want to live today,
if I were going to die tomorrow.
I'm not impressed by the future.
Perhaps death will be a warm rain
on the lake surface.

Although the outer seeds
Have been picked and shattered
By starlings, the sunflower heads
Hang heavy on the stalks, battered
In the sudden rain, ice, snow.

Their empty seed beds, eyes of giant insects,
Stare down on the mutilated rows
Of garden. Granular snow collects
Between the hard calyx ribs and flows
Like salt on the frozen ground below.

Behind them, the ravaged spindles
Of corn grind and rasp in the wind.
The garden whitens; everything dwindles
In size, except these giants lined
Up against the encroaching snow.

If I had built a high path
Around this garden, I would walk,
Morning and evening, and watch the wrath
Of rising winds, the writhing stalks,
The flat victory of snow.

Peter MacLean Stevens

POEM FOR ERNIE LO

I am watching Ernest paint. His
Oriental fingers, steadying
The sable brush, drift
Between watercolour trees
That grow like misted dreams
On sheets of paper towel.

Bamboo shoots up;
Islands stare back at me
Like ancestors. Millenial tradition
Flows from his fingertips
Into quiet pools upon the page.

Oh no, he says, I make mistake.
Ernie, what does it matter to me
That bamboo leaves point up in Spring,
Not down?

Lois Simmie

Sister
there are just the two of us
and I don't see you enough.
Must we talk about your hair
and your neighbour's shag carpet
and your children and your house?

Do you ever feel joy so fierce
that the grey days are worthwhile?
Is being grown up anything like you
expected it to be? wanted it to be?
Do you think of the night our father died
and we were not there
because the doctor said to go home
and get some rest . . . and we went?
Do you think about that?

I always think the next time we meet
it will be different.
But we will talk about
draperies or slipcovers,
furniture or fashions.

Sister
do you ever think that the
last words we say to each other
might be about
your new bathroom paper?

Elizabeth Allen

MR PODDLE

Mr Poddle the postman
waddles into view
his plimsolls lop lopping
along on the footpath

He's bringing me letters
from country cousins
telling me
  how good it is
  living free back
  to nature
and that Bunky Harris
finally married the sea witch
who lives in the sand dunes

I phone Aunt Maude
to tell her the news
my fingers impatiently
tip tapping on the notepad
where my pen has been doodling
postmen with tan/black
caterpillars crawling
fuzz/haired between
their toes

But when he comes to the door
I am afraid
he will winkle
his way inside
  before I
sweep up the corpses
that lie on the floor
Sweep them under the carpet
(for future reference)

Hearing his knock
I hurry and change
into my evening skin
so he won't catch me
looking old and wrinkled

"Ahhh! but I'm crazy about you
Mr Poddle," I say
weaving my warm plump hands
through his mousy hair
and he curls up
on my lap pressing
his nose into the marigolds
I wear on my lapel
and we sip tea
on my breezy verandah
his bag of letters
forgotten at my feet

PORTRAIT

When I brought you
  blindfolded and crated
  in dusty teachests
to the grey-brown prairie
I did not know
you had secreted
a trumpet shell
into your flax kitbag

and that at night
  you would listen
  to the sea whispering

When you left
I could not stop
the blood flowing
from the gaping wound
left inside of me

and when I opened
the first-aid-kit
I found only sea sponges
which I bound on
with the torn sheets
of our marriage bed

In dreams
I paint thoughts of you
which the chill morning
                sweeps away

I tried to bring you back
by painting wildflowers
  in your hands
and sending crocuses
packed in barley husks
hoping you would remember,
  the sweet smell of clover
  crushed honey perfume
    beneath our bodies
    on warm summer evenings

Now I stand
in front of your unfinished portrait
trying to stop my hand
from painting a seascape
        behind you

With tight closed eyes
      I picture
the colour of wheatfields
    and you,
standing by the barn door
  warm summernight wind
  wrapping around your body,
gazing far out on the prairie
wistful for the sea

John V. Hicks

THREE KERNELS OF PARCHED CORN

I have lost you, winged one; you have flown,
leaving me with three kernels of parched corn
and the memory of a lure laid at evening
from the edge of the wood to this
as I thought
point of union. When at last you emerged
I watched my offering grain by spaced grain
drawing you closer. You were very near,
three grains distant only,
when the sound rose, the whirr of flight
and the thousand voices, the migration
calling, calling you to come. The flock
was brilliant in the blue air, the sky
sang with thanksgivings. Now
I am left three kernels of parched corn
and this patch of grey light
by which I press them
one by one into the cold ground.

THE SPEECH OF YOUR COUNTRY

The speech of your country is like music,
resisting translation, sufficient of itself
in phrase and cadence, flowing eloquently towards
the perfect understanding. You walk beside me
a stranger, yet at the touch of hand and hand
words rest upon the tongue, needless
of being spoken. It is like light
kindled at morning, like song's unburdening
from the first outlined tree.

They will ask why
I come silent from my journey, why I bring
no message, no least token; and I shall say,
the speech of her country is like music
not to be translated, sense of its own sound,
entire with meaning. Set adrift in the heart,
it finds the ear in its own fashion. I
have heard it, and I understand.

WHERE YOU BEGIN LIKE RIVERS

Where you begin like rivers
I hear a sweet singing;
the little stones have voices.
I and the flood tide
are one; we gather and rush on together
under the steepled mountain; we are flying
horses that leap and thunder and are thrown
over a brink and far
out, far down, far on
into a tranquillity of waters;
and faint through the ensuing silence I
hear again the small rock voices,
the sweet singing,
where you begin like rivers.

THE MORNING OF THE MINOR SCALES

The pigeon lying on its side in the lane,
wings folded, blue tints reflecting the sun,
accepts the impartiality of death with dignity.
The overhead wire it broke its neck on

hums softly as though with messages:
there will be no more strutting on rooftops, no
climbing high above the city on romping winds.

Morning faces appearing at back windows
yawn, pale eyes above stubblebeards assess
the possibilities of a day like other days.

A street cleaner, stopping his pushcart, taking
note of the still form, the closed eye, selects
a tool appropriate to an unaccustomed mortician.

A small girl in pink, swinging a music case,
yellow hair brushed shining, pauses, stares
for a still moment, one foot in air, before
she trips away humming a sombre sequence,
confident of her newly mastered minor scales.

BY NIGHT, LOOKING DOWN

Head downwards
this fearful height
above the glittering spear tips of
                    armies endlessly marching
far and far below,
I, a particle,
magnetized, dare I hope, permanently,
utter a prayer
by night, looking down
through the terrible dark, suspended
above the glittering spear points of
                    armies endlessly marching:
Hold fast, earth, mother lode,
do not release me;
hold fast,
do not let go.

THE SENSE OF AN ENDING

There were three that witnessed the burial; a gaunt crow,
a squirrel snipping fruit from conifers, a fox,
name for a shadow, poised lightly as thought,
drawn by the nostrils to this consignation.
Only the crow, preserving
some semblance of solemnity, could be said
to have considered the facts; the squirrel at its bitter meal
held aloof by hunger, the shadow form savouring the air
one foot indexed for flight, by these
were significances ignored, indifference and uncertainty
unwittingly combined. But the crow will fly
forever just out of reach of our regrets, not quite absent,
never intruding, a symbol of the passing of all things,
a presence against the sun, the sense of an ending.

Fate was our absent witness; it knew
what we could not know, that for the unspoken complaint
there was no ear. We heard only
intrusion of the smallest sound, the bare break
of silence as rejected scale particles
spun to the forest floor. The impressed footstep
of curiosity, inaudible, passed, scarcely
a movement of air. A black wing was to hold
our only relevance in the impassive earth's
slow spindle. It was a proper ending. It asked
what could the birth be but this; the upsurge
but the implicity, the subsiding?

Lala Koehn

MY TEA PARTY

behind me, the river looks murky and grey
the gulls shrill call and
low sweeping wings are touching the ground.
it rains
        I sit in my salmon coloured chair,
        with its stiff Victorian back,
        proper,
        ladylike and
        sad
for the colour of the velvet does not match my skin at all
and it is also tea time
        and this is when I do remember
        I have just the perfect thing
        for my lovely velvet chair.
I bring in my three goldeye
I have readied for the pan and I
seat them in my chair
with their matching salmonskins
        asking them to be my guests,
        serving crumpets, jam and cake
and we all have a lovely visit,
sipping tea, watching the rain

THE SKY LARK

I knew it would be there
suspended motionless staining the sky
and it looks like that black ink spot
that I spilled on my ruffled, pale blue dress
when my friends called after me: "look
there comes again the starched baby doll!"
and suddenly
it breaks out into a song
its voice trembling and quivering
the sound bouncing off my open palms
spilling like glass beads into the grainfield
and I dig and dig
and search for it in the black soil
between the fine hairy roots

I pick an armful of red poppies
and cornflowers
and run in my bare feet
to the grove of trees and the hidden brook
where the daisies and kingcups
and forget-me-nots grow
to weave a wreath for my hair
and chains upon chains of sowthistle
for my neck and arms
and I bow and wave graciously
my fan of plumaged fern
at the mushrooms and blackberries
my faithful subjects
and walk down the balk taking dainty steps
to the thatched cottage
knock at the door and say:

"niech bedzie pochwalony Jesus Chrystus"
"n wieki wiekow" the woman answers
bidding me welcome   asks me to sit down
on the cleanly scrubbed bench
"Jasio, fetch a dipper of buttermilk
our little miss is here"
and she unwraps a linencovered
freshly baked loaf
murmuring "w imie Ojca i Syna"
her knife traces the Sign of the Cross
cuts through the crust
and she watches me eat
the butter melting, running down my chin

"and who are we today?" she asks
and smiles, looking at my splendid, long chains
and my flowerdecked hair
"I am Princess Forget-me-not
and I thank you kindly for your hospitality" I answer
hiding the end of the crust in my pinafore pocket

Mildred A. Rose

AUGUST DUST

August dust is warm
to my bare feet.
My thin cotton dress clings
wetly to my five-year old body.
Against the hot morning sun
something is moving
along the trail from the creek,
something is moving
between heads
of stiffly ripened wheat.

Ears pricked,
sharp nose
snuffling the dust
Coyote is trotting
toward me, I pick up
a stick and wait.
He does not look at me
but slips back of the barn
where yesterday, Father tossed
an old rooster onto the manure pile.

Coyote seizes the dead bird
and races back
along the trail from the creek
between heads
of stiffly ripened wheat.
He passes me.
His golden-yellow eyes
glare with hunger
beyond the perimeter
of my experience.

Mother calls, "Breakfast!"
Coyote blends silently,
easily into the August dust.

H. C. Dillow

WINTER MOUSE

Twenty below it was
When we found him in the garage,
In the old bin
Where we keep the grain we scatter to birds
On winter mornings,
Skittering round over the shifting surface
Like young thoughts in an old man's brain,
Replete to a roundness
But leaping desperately for the bin's edge
A good six inches above his head,
Eye-buttons dark with fear,
Stretching on feet delicate as ice ferns
On a frosted pane.

Our four gloved hands to reach him out,
Cold, and afraid of squeezing too hard,
Amazed at the quickness
Of the small life under the fur,
At the string tail
And the gloriously extravagant ears.
Then, abruptly still, curled for a moment
In a leather palm –
Up, over the edge,
And down, scuttling into shadows,
Barely touching the frozen earth of the floor.

Hands numb with cold
We fumbled with books and car keys
As we'd fumbled with that living quicksilver
In the bin a moment before,
And questioned the morning light
For tokens of a thaw –
Having learned the value of such minor portents
When mice and lovers bide a precarious season
Sharing a cold edge for balance –
For signs that this day at least
Would keep some measure in its rougher weather,
And keep our lives together.

John G. Trehas

Yellow hen of sun
Pecks at the grains of dewdrops
On the morning grass

Peter Huston

MOTHER AND DAUGHTER

In the dark green hospital corridor
they sat, mother and daughter,
and the syllables
of talk and laughter
slipped to and fro,
the lap of waves on stones,
in the soft and liquid
language of the Crees,
whose thoughts are formed
to the sounding of a cool breeze
across a thousand miles of water,
through a million trees.

J. A. Krause

DUCK EGGS

I find them in burnt grass
still warm creamheavy round
each tortoise-coloured shell
in place

(there will be fourteen
holes in my sky)

MY CHILD

My child
gathers crickets
(wounded and whole)
and plants

them
under her window
to sing her
into night

suckled
by the hurl
of wind-torn hawk
she knows

no easy sleep

JOHN MORRIS

John Morris (out
in his slippers
without his teeth)
inched up to
idling cars to
knock on windows

he whispered
he wanted a ride
to go
somewhere
with all the people
going somewhere,
going somewhere
else

Catherine M. Buckaway

CROWS

A black pillar of crows
Rises like dusky smoke
From a far-off place on this land.

Where even
The stones
Consume one another.

When they wheel no longer overhead
To break their separate raucous cries,
I know the crows are feasting.

Beside an old animal skull,
A mouse flicks into the sunlight.
The earth swallows his colour.

Air blackened with the surge of wings
Spread for wind and upward lunge
Into infinite sky. There the birds

Will ascend, flaying one another,
Cawing their loud cries through all space
Their bodies defying wind.

STRANGELY THE BIRDS HAVE COME

I, frozen have turned inside my years
as the sun turns
inside the changing day.
I look beyond my image
to find that the natural world makes sense.

Strangely the birds have come,
and I hold my ears against their song of summer.
Branches yield red-lipped flowers
to soften the hardness of this landscape,
fires flow in the lichened rocks
and in their fine ash nothing can escape.

Washes of gold cleanse the threshold of my imagination
and catch the cadence of my outward dreams:
I find myself gliding through the shadows
while the present unravels in a torn web around me.

TWO CHOICES

I ask you to try again
and give me a different life to lead:
only in shame grows
confusion, large and dissolving.

I watch you dancing on muskeg
(clutter of roots
and vegetable decay);
in the grey half-light
you drift down past
rows of cedars
that shed deeply on stone.

Now at least I have two clear choices,
to follow a song
vanishing in the wind;
or to stay where I am,
stiff in old antagonisms
and my face melting off like wax.

A GIFT OF GREAT VALUE

Listen to the morning bring forth
the power of a wakened prairie.
Feel gardens changing;
a rapture:
through the eyes
see little explosions of green
in sunlit corners.

Full faced winter
has dissolved in one moment,
corrupting
the certainty of death.

Through my soft skull
hawks escape to plough the air.
A crone, with a hook nose
and foul skin,
frequently interrupts
these arrangements.

I dream daily
that I catch lightning
and lead it underground.

Prudently
I know how to distinguish
dreams from truth;
and how to distinguish
that which lives in light
from that which steps over the edge
into growing darkness.

Time is haloed
in this new world:
I nourish gladness
and walk with fluid limbs
through the silence
of the red earth.

NOTES ON THE CONTRIBUTORS

MARK ABLEY is from Saskatoon and is studying in England at Oxford. He has published in periodicals, and has one chapbook, *The Cutting Edge.*
ELIZABETH ALLEN grew up in New Zealand on a farm near the sea. She came to the prairies in 1972, and lives on a mixed farm near Lemberg. Her poems have appeared in periodicals.
BYRNA BARCLAY was born in Saskatoon and now lives in Regina. Byrna writes poems, stories, and has finished a novel, *Summer of the Hungry Pup,* parts of which have been published.
ELIZABETH BREWSTER was born in Chipman, New Brunswick. She has lived in many parts of Canada and has been in Saskatoon for five years, teaching English at the University of Saskatchewan. Besides widespread periodical publication, she has published four books of poetry, the most recent being *Sometimes I Think of Moving,* a novel, *The Sisters,* and a collection of short stories, *It's Easy to fall on the Ice* (all with Oberon).
CATHERINE M. BUCKAWAY was born in North Battleford and now lives in Saskatoon. Besides extensive periodical publication, she has three books of poetry, the most recent of which is *The Silver Cuckoo* (Borealis).
MICK BURRS came to Canada (from California) in 1965, to Saskatchewan in 1971. He writes poems, plays, stories, and songs. As well as several chapbooks with his own Waking Image Press, Mick has a longer book, *Moving in from Paradise* (Thunder Creek Co-op).
MARTHA C. CRAWFORD lives in Carrot River. Her poems have appeared in periodicals.
ROBERT CURRIE grew up in Moose Jaw, where he lives with his wife and two children. Following several chapbooks, his book *Diving into Fire* was published by Oberon in 1977. Bob founded *Salt* magazine, which he has edited for eight years.
H. C. DILLOW was born in New York City and came to Canada in 1961. He teaches at the University of Regina, where he has also edited the *Wascana Review.* His poems have appeared in many periodicals.
E. F. DYCK was born in Turnhill. He studied philosophy and mathematical logic, "from which it was a natural progression to poetry." His poems have appeared on CBC *Anthology* and in periodicals. A book will soon be published with Thunder Creek Co-op.
DENNIS GRUENDING was born in St. Benedict, where he spent time as a "German Catholic farmboy." He now works as a CBC producer and newsman in Regina; his poems have been published in several periodicals.
TERRENCE HEATH was born in Regina and now lives in the country near Saskatoon. He has published poems and stories in periodicals, and one book, *The Truth and Other Stories* with Anansi; another book, *Touchwood* (Turnstone Press) will appear soon.
JOHN V. HICKS was born in London, England, but grew up in western Canada "in the reign of George V." He has been an accountant, organist, and choirmaster. His poems have been read on CBC *Anthology* and have been widely published in periodicals.

PETER HUSTON is "a middle-aged physician with a large family." Originally from England, Peter now lives in Regina. He began writing poems after forty.

GARY HYLAND was born in Moose Jaw where he still lives, teaching English at Riverview Collegiate. His poems have appeared in many periodicals, and he has two chapbooks, *Poems From a Loft* (Sundog) and *Home Street* (Thunder Creek Co-op).

AUDREY JOHANNESSOHN recently hitch-hiked back to Saskatchewan from British Columbia, because she wanted to write about her home province. She now lives in Lloydminster.

DON KERR was born in Saskatoon, where he teaches English at the University of Saskatchewan. His poems have appeared in periodicals, and he is an associate editor of *Grain.*

LALA KOEHN has lived on the prairies for twenty years, but has recently been transplanted to Victoria. As well as periodical publications and exhibitions of her paintings, she has a chapbook with Thistledown Press, *Portraits.*

J. A. KRAUSE was born in Regina, where she is now teaching. Her poems have appeared in a number of periodicals.

JAMES L. McLEAN was born in Moose Jaw, where he still lives, working for the CPR as a railway carman. He has published poems and fiction, and did the line drawings for Prairie Books' *Wild Flowers Across the Prairies.*

JAMES MacNEILL was born in North Battleford, and grew up in Kerrobert. His poems have appeared in numerous periodicals and he has a book *Prairiefire* (Western Extension College). He has also edited three short story anthologies with Glen Sorestad.

RONALD MARKEN grew up in Camrose, Alberta, and has taught at the University of Saskatchewan (Saskatoon) since 1966. He has published poems, articles, and reviews in periodicals, and has a chapbook, *Dark Honey,* with Thistledown Press. He also edited an anthology of prison writing, *Don't Steal This Book* (Green Tree Publishing).

KEN MITCHELL was born in Moose Jaw and now teaches English at the University of Regina. Ken has many periodical publications, as well as a novel, *Wandering Rafferty,* and a book of short stories, *Everybody Gets Something Here*. He has also published *The Meadowlark Connection* with Pile o' Bones Press.

GARRY RADDYSH was born in Kamsack and is now teaching English in Churchbridge. His poems have appeared in several periodicals.

R. E. RASHLEY was born in Leicester, England and came to Canada when he was two. Besides periodical publications, he published four chapbooks, the most recent being *Paso por aqui* (Fiddlehead), and one critical work, *Poetry in Canada: The First Three Steps* (Ryerson). He died in 1975.

RALPH RING was born in Moose Jaw and now lives in the country near Stony Beach. His poems have appeared in several periodicals.

MILDRED A. ROSE was born in Pike Lake and now lives in Regina. She has published poems, stories, and reviews in numerous periodicals, and has two chapbooks, *Esor Derdlim* and *Second Story* (Music House).

BARBARA SAPERGIA is from Moose Jaw and now lives in Regina. Poems and stories have appeared in several periodicals, and she is writing a novel.
STEPHEN SCRIVER was born in Wolseley, where he worked on his father's weekly newspaper. He now teaches in Grenfell. His book of hockey poems, *Between the Lines,* will appear soon (Thistledown Press).
NANCY SENIOR came to Saskatchewan in 1968. She teaches at the University of Saskatchewan (Saskatoon). She has numerous periodical publications, as well as two chapbooks: *Poems* and *I Never Wanted to be the Holy Ghost* (both Fiddlehead).
LOIS SIMMIE grew up in Mervin and Livelong and now lives in Saskatoon. She has published stories and poems and has completed a novel. She has taught creative writing at the Saskatchewan School of the Arts.
GLEN SORESTAD was born in Vancouver, but moved to the prairies when he was ten. He has published poems and stories extensively, and has three books of poems, including *Prairie Pub Poems* and *Wind Songs* with Thistledown Press. He also co-edited (with James MacNeill) three short story anthologies.
BARRY STEVENS was born in Ottawa, was a journalist and businessman, then returned to school. He studied education and became a kindergarten teacher in Moose Jaw.
PETER MacLEAN STEVENS was born in Moose Jaw and is now studying English at the University of Saskatchewan.
ANDREW SUKNASKI was born and raised in Wood Mountain. He is currently writer-in-residence at the University of Manitoba. Andy has extensive periodical publications, numerous chapbooks, under his own Sundog imprint and with Repository Press, and a book with Macmillan, *Wood Mountain Poems.* He also has a chapbook of Sioux children's stories with Thistledown Press, and a new book of poems forthcoming from Macmillan.
ANNE SZUMIGALSKI came to Saskatoon from London, England, in 1951. As well as extensive periodical publications, Anne has a book, *Woman Reading in Bath,* with Doubleday. She is an associate editor of *Grain* and has taught at the Saskatchewan School of the Arts.
LUETTA TREHAS was born in Tompkins and lives now in Regina. Her poetry and short stories have appeared in many periodicals and on CBC radio.
JOHN G. TREHAS, a Canadian of Greek descent, lives in Regina. His poems have appeared in many periodicals.
LORNA UHER is from Swift Current. She has published in many periodicals and has one chapbook, *Inside is the Sky* (Thistledown Press). Lorna has also taught at the Saskatchewan School of the Arts.
GEOFFREY URSELL was born in Moose Jaw and now teaches part-time at the University of Regina. His poems have been published in periodicals and his songs appeared in *Singin' About Us* (Lorimer). His play, *The Running of the Deer*, is the 1977 Clifford E. Lee winner, and a story, *Radio Waves,* has been broadcast on CBC *Anthology.*
DAVID WALTNER-TOEWS was born in Winnipeg, now lives in Saskatoon, has a degree in English, and is studying veterinary medicine. He has published poems and stories in various periodicals.

ACKNOWLEDGEMENTS

Poems included in *Number One Northern* have previously appeared in the following places and are used by permission as indicated. Mark Abley: *New Statesman, The Green and White,* reprinted by permission of the author. Elizabeth Allen: *CV/II*, reprinted by permission of the author. Byrna Barclay: reprinted by permission of the author. Poems by Elizabeth Brewster from *Sunrise North* are reprinted by permission of Clarke, Irwin, & Company Limited. Catherine M. Buckaway: CBC *Anthology, Strangely the Birds have Come* (Fiddlehead Poetry Books), *Wascana Review*, reprinted by permission of the author. Mick Burrs: CBC *Anthology, Moving in from Paradise* (Thunder Creek Co-Op), reprinted by permission of the author. Martha C. Crawford: *Grain*, reprinted by permission of the author. Robert Currie: CBC *Anthology, Halls of Elsinore* (Sesame Press), *Moving Out* (Thunder Creek Co-op), reprinted by permission of the author; poems from *Diving into Fire* are reprinted by permission of the author and Oberon Press. H.C. Dillow: *Grain,* reprinted by permission of the author. E.F. Dyck: *CV/II, The North Shore Review, Salt,* reprinted by permission of the author. Dennis Greunding: *Grain,* reprinted by permission of the author. Terrence Heath: CBC *Anthology,* reprinted by permission of the author. John V. Hicks: CBC *Anthology, Dalhousie Review, Grain, Mademoiselle, New York Herald Tribune, Wascana Review,* reprinted by permission of the author. Peter Huston: reprinted by permission of the author. Gary Hyland: CBC *Anthology, Home Street* (Thunder Creek Co-op), *Horizon* (Oxford University Press), reprinted by permission of the author. Audrey Johannessohn: reprinted by permission of the author. Don Kerr: reprinted by permission of the author. Lala Koehn: *Grain,* reprinted by permission of the author. J.A. Krause: *Salt,* reprinted by permission of the author. James L. McLean: *Grain, Salt,* reprinted by permission of the author. James MacNeill, *Prairiefire* (Western Extension College), reprinted by permission of the author. Ronald Marken: *Dark Honey* (Thistledown Press), reprinted by permission of the author. Ken Mitchell: *Canadian Forum, Smoke Signals,* reprinted by permission of the author. Garry Raddysh: *Grain, Salt*, reprinted by permission of the author. R.E. Rashley: *Paso por aqui* (Fiddlehead Poetry Books), reprinted by permission of Laura Rashley.Ralph Ring: *Grain,* reprinted by permission of the author. Mildred A. Rose: *Salt,* reprinted by permission of the author. Barbara Sapergia: *Grain, NeWest Review, Smoke Signals,* reprinted by permission of the author. Stephen Scriver: *Between the Lines* (Thistledown Press), reprinted by permission of the author. Nancy Senior: *Grain, I Never Wanted to be the Holy Ghost* (Fiddlehead Poetry Books), reprinted by permission of the author. Lois Simmie: *Salt,* reprinted by permission of the author. Glen Sorestad: CBC *Anthology, Prairie Pub Poems, Wind Songs* (Thistledown Press), reprinted by permission of the author. Barry Stevens: *Salt,* reprinted by permission of the author. Peter MacLean Stevens: reprinted by permission of the author. Poems from *Wood Mountain Poems* by *Andrew Suknaski* are reprinted by permission of The Macmillan Company of Canada Limited: the version of "Indian Rings at the Edge of Tonita

Pasture" – first section – is reprinted by special permission of the author and any further reprints are to be taken from *Wood Mountain Poems*; the other poem is reprinted by permission of the author. "It Wasn't A Major Operation," "Long Distance," "Nettles," and "A Celebration," which originally appeared in *Salt* are all from the book *Woman Reading in Bath*, copyright © 1974 by Anne Szumigalski. These poems are reprinted by permission of Doubleday & Company, Inc. Other poems by Anne Szumigalski appeared in *Saskatoon Poets '74* and are reprinted by permission of the author. Luetta Trehas: *The Fiddlehead*, reprinted by permission of the author. John G. Trehas: reprinted by permission of the author. Lorna Uher, CBC *Anthology, Grain, Horizon* (Oxford University Press), *Inside is the Sky* (Thistledown Press), *Malahat Review, Salt*, reprinted by permission of the author. Geoffrey Ursell: *CV/II Canadian Forum, Homegrown , 1977 Giant Canadian Poetry Annual* (Press Porcepic), reprinted by permission of the author. David Waltner-Toews: *Canadian Forum, Prism International*, reprinted by permission of the author.

The Thunder Creek Co-op is a production co-operative registered with the Saskatchewan Department of Co-operation and Co-operative Development. It was formed to publish prairie writing – poetry, prose, plays, and song.

OTHER PUBLICATIONS

GHOST HOUSE, stories and poems by Lois Simmie (with photographs c. 1910)	$3.00
MOVING IN FROM PARADISE, poems by Mick Burrs	$3.00
HOME STREET, poems by Gary Hyland	$1.25
MOVING OUT, poems by Robert Currie	$1.25
PRAIRIE GRASS, PRAIRIE SKY, an lp with songs by Rob Bryanton, Bob Evans, Glenn Koudelka, Connie Kaldor, and Geoffrey Ursell; distributed by the Thunder Creek Co-op	$5.50

FORTHCOMING

A collection of Saskatchewan short stories, edited by Robert Kroetsch

A first collection of poems by E. F. Dyck

All of the above may be ordered from

Thunder Creek Co-op
1188 Duffield Crescent
Moose Jaw, Saskatchewan